Bully

Prevention Tips for Teens

Bully

Prevention Tips for Teens

18 Powerful Ways to Protect Yourself through High School

Yvonne Brooks and
Stephanie R. Bien, LMFT, LPCC

BULLY PREVENTION TIPS FOR TEENS
18 POWERFUL WAYS TO PROTECT YOURSELF THROUGH HIGH SCHOOL

iUniverse books may be ordered through booksellers or by contacting:

iUniverse
1663 Liberty Drive
Bloomington, IN 47403
www.iuniverse.com
1-800-Authors (1-800-288-4677)

ISBN: 978-1-5320-0769-9 (sc)
ISBN: 978-1-5320-0768-2 (e)

Library of Congress Control Number: 2016916669

Print information available on the last page.

iUniverse rev. date: 10/26/2016

*A percentage of the proceeds from book sales will be donated to Chai Lifeline, helping seriously ill children and their families to have a happy and normal childhood.

Yvonne's Dedication

This is book is dedicated to an amazing young lady I met years ago when she was in the eighth grade. This young lady inspired me greatly to write and publish materials to empower teenagers toward reaching their highest potential. It's an honor to see Nayiri all grown up and entering medical school this year. I am so proud of you! The value you've added to my life and the Brooks & Brooks Foundation is priceless! Love you.

Stephanie's Dedication

I dedicate this book to my own teen daughters Rebecca and Jessica and to all the teens around the world and in future generations. I wholeheartedly impart these 18 lessons to bring peace and joy to the individual and have faith that this will help to make the world a better place.

Acknowledgements

We would like to thank the 500 students who anonymously took the survey, Ms. Kolker, El Camino High School, Kirby Welsh, Calabasas High School for letting us come in and speak to their students. We also would like to thank Jeff Gerson, Assistant Principal at a LAUSD school and our editors Lori Nelson and Jane Purden.

Foreword

Why do they insult me and call me names all the time?
Why do they talk behind my back?
Why do they spread rumors about me?
Why do they ignore me when I walk by?
Why are they so mean?
What did I do to deserve this?

These are questions many of us ask ourselves. Whether we're high school students, employees in a hostile work environment, or in an abusive personal relationship, bullying is a challenge that many face.

While this book is geared towards teenagers, there is wisdom in it for us all! In this **One Of a Kind Book**, two knowledgeable and inspirational women that I have been honored to work with, provide tips, inspiration, and practical activities to address these questions and the challenge of bullying.

When I was asked to write the foreword for this **Ground Breaking Book**, I was not only deeply humbled, but hit with flashbacks from many bullying related situations I endured throughout my life:

> ....kids at school taunting me because of my height, weight, or religious background

....a grey haired, cane wielding, ex-military father standing beside me on the back lawn teaching me hand to hand combat techniques to fight off the neighborhood bullies.

....getting sent to the principal's office for beating up the bully

....people in work settings spreading false rumors about myself and others

As a teacher, assistant principal, and principal for a large urban school district for the last 25 years, I have observed and intervened in countless bullying situations. Many of these experiences contributed to my selection as the 2011-2012 Assistant Principal of the Year for the Los Angeles Chapter of the California Association of School Administrators. Guiding my own three children through years of bullying issues has given me added perspective and appreciation of the value of this book.

I wish I had this book back then to give guidance to my students, teachers, and my own children. The many tips, problem-solution approach, practice activities and inspirational quotes would have helped many children and makes it a **Must-Have book** for counselors, teachers, teenagers, and parents! The activities enhance and complement many school districts' Bullying Prevention, Conflict Resolution, and Social Emotional Learning (SEL) programs.

Merging a wide range and long history of experiences, the authors crafted their years of wisdom and knowledge into this anti-bully-bible. **Yvonne Brooks** has worked for over 25 years developing programs in the US and abroad to empower parents and teens to manage many of life's challenges. She currently heads the Brooks and Brooks Foundation in the Los Angeles Area, a non-profit organization that serves, educates, and empowers families toward living with purpose.

For over 20 years, **Stephanie Bien** has been supporting children, teenagers, and families as a licensed Marriage, Family and Child therapist and "Parent Effectiveness Trainer". She has led numerous workshops for both parents and children. Stephanie has been actively involved with many community programs supporting youth and teens.

Jeff Gerson
Educator and Parent

Introduction

"Bullying" is not a new societal issue. We can go back in time and see that people have been hurting one another for centuries. There are stories in the Bible of the struggles between Esau and Jacob, Joseph and his brothers, Sodom and Gomorrah. We have a history of battles, wars and the Holocaust. All very tumultuous times, but the word bullying wasn't used throughout history.

Not until we got to the time of insight and expression of feelings did we take matters more seriously. In 1999 the Columbine shooting shed light on to a serious problem. Along with broadcasting and Internet, more situations came to our attention. We now are able to see that bullying was an enormous societal problem. In the years to follow, we see teens reacting either by shooting at the school, committing suicide or homicide, or other less severe measures, but experiencing pain nonetheless.

We decided to write this book to offer a deeper personal understanding and personal tools to empower, heal and grow for both the bully and the victim. The bottom line is that it's about the struggle with self-esteem, self-doubt and negative thoughts that perpetuate the cycle of bullying.

As we set out to write this book, we surveyed 500 teens from 8th to 12th grade. 49% surveyed said they have been bullied. We knew this number was low. What we saw was the need for a definition. Many reported that they had not been bullied when in fact according to our definition, they had been. After defining it, the number increased to 98% of teens have either lost sleep, missed days of school or spoke to an authority figure (school counselor, parent, principal or vice principal) about an issue that they didn't know how to handle. So let's spend a few minutes defining what "bullying" is.

I interviewed my colleague and friend Deputy Alicia Kohno from the Sheriff's station, Juvenile Prevention Program, otherwise known as the J-team. She stated, "Bullying is imposing on someone else with threat or potential harm." Bullying comes in many forms. The statistics we came up with included physical bullying which was 32.53%, emotional bullying at 71.98%, verbal bullying 84.27% and cyber bullying at 51.81%.

Physical Bullying is hitting, pushing, kicking, fighting, but in my opinion can include the use of power of a larger teen that is feared because of size. This can also comprise of physical property being taken or damaged in someway. In our survey, this type of bullying occurred at lower levels of frequency but nonetheless this is a very damaging form of retaliation causing either to feel extreme fear and threat. These young people tend to be fearful of going to school and fear for their safety.

Emotional Bullying is ignoring or excluding others in activities or relationships, threatening, insulting or mocking, humiliating, intimidating or any other way that degrades another and hurts their self-esteem. This is a common theme in middle and high schools. These teens also struggle with self-esteem.

Verbal Bullying was reported to occur most frequently. The definition is "using words in negative ways such as insults, teasing, put downs, etc., to gain power over someone else's life". This can feel devastating to the person who is being bullied, making them feel uncomfortable and awkward in situations. These teens struggle with going to school and may have trouble fitting in. Verbal abuse is very similar to the above, emotional abuse.

Cyberbullying tends to occur more frequently than reported. This definition is to bully another online by sending or posting mean, hurtful, or intimidating messages. Sometimes this is done anonymously.

Each and every one of us, young and old, struggle with self-esteem issues, self-doubt and negative thoughts. Some have acquired more tools than others to cope and to get back on track. This book is designed to empower you with tools to heal and grow. It doesn't mean that after going through the chapters and doing the exercises, that you will then feel good. What it means is "this is a start to learn helpful tools so that when you're feeling low, you can go back to using them when needed. It's a work in progress, as is LIFE."

Bully Statistics

Research suggests that being bullied has similar and in some cases worse long-term adverse effects on young adults' mental health than being maltreated (Lereya, Copeland, Costello & Wolke, 2015).

School-based bully prevention programs decreased bullying by up to 25% (McCallion & Feder, 2013).

Almost all forms of bullying peak in middle school and then decrease in tenth grade (Zweig, Dank, Lachman, & Yahner, 2013).

Students who experience bullying are at increased risk for depression, anxiety, sleep difficulties and poor school adjustment (Center for Disease Control 2012).

In general, incidents of bullying were higher among males than females and higher in 6th grade through 8th grade students than 9th grade through 10th (American Medical Association, 2001).

Approximately 43% of middle school student's reports experiencing cyberbullying during their lifetime (Patchin, 2015).

Cyberbullying has negative effects on victims, such as lowering self-esteem, increasing depression and producing feelings of powerlessness (Anderson, Bresnahan, & Musatics, 2014).

Table of Contents

TIP #1

Believe in Yourself

You are perfect just the way you are!

We are all unique human beings with different characteristics, qualities and skills that make us who we are. If we believe in ourselves, we can do anything. We need to accept our specialness, and realize that our soul is ours alone. We can feel good about our personal gifts. These are the qualities that we bring to our environment – to our homes, our schools and our groups of friends and loved ones. We each have our purpose in life that we are here to share with the world.

This confidence and self-love shines outwards and spreads to others. Confidence and self-love are also repellants to being picked on or bullied. A bully doesn't tend to pick on someone that shines happiness. And if they try, the negativity doesn't go in, it gets deflected.

One of my favorite stories is about a holy man named Zusya who lay crying on his deathbed. His disciples asked their teacher, "Why are you so sad? After all the good deeds you have done, you will surely get a great reward in heaven!"

"I'm afraid!" said Zusya. "Because when I get to heaven, I know God's not going to ask me, 'Why weren't you more like Moses?' or 'Why weren't you more like King David?' But I'm afraid that God will ask 'Zusya, why weren't you more like Zusya?' And then what will I say?!"

What a great message for us – we are all here to do our part as our exclusive selves.

"Believing in Yourself" Questions to Ponder:

1. What are some characteristics about yourself that you are proud of?
2. How can you enhance your good qualities?
3. What makes you, you?
4. If you could improve one skill, what would it be?
5. What makes you unique?

Solution

Why don't we believe in ourselves sometimes?

We may feel insecure about fitting in. Or we may look at the next person, comparing ourselves to who they are rather than seeing that we are perfect just the way we are.

But we can just as easily gravitate to the good in ourselves, follow the positive, and be who we want to be. We can admire our own uniqueness and admire that in others rather than falling victim to judgments.

Be the person that you want to be and believe in yourself!

Quotes

"If you believe in yourself and feel confident in yourself, you can do anything. I really believe that."
~Karlie Kloss

"I don't want to be the cliché American Idol dude. I want to be different, you know - that's the whole goal, me and music. It's about being yourself and being unique."
~Paul McDonald

"Friends can help each other. A true friend is someone who lets you have total freedom to be yourself - and especially to feel. Or, not to feel. Whatever you happen to be feeling at the moment is fine with them. That's what real love amounts to - letting a person be what he really is."
~Jim Morrison

"I gave up my struggle with perfection a long time ago. That is a concept I don't find very interesting anymore. Everyone just wants to look good in the photographs. I think that is where some of the pressure comes from. Be happy. Be yourself, the day is about a lot more."
~Anne Hathaway

Practice

Please think about the questions below, and then write the answers. This will give you insights and possibly a new perspective to seeing others and yourself.

1. List 3 people that you don't like and then write a positive character trait that they have.

       <u>Person</u>   <u>Trait</u>

   1.

   2.

   3.

2. List 5 qualities that make you special.

   1.

   2.

   3.

   4.

   5.

Journal

To be myself I will…

The way that I'll expand on my special qualities is…

 Yvonne Brooks and Stephanie R. Bien, LMFT, LPCC

TIP #2

Align With Your Purpose for Life

Would you rather achieve average results by doing what you think is right or would you rather be successful as a result of working at your highest potential?

The difference between these two paths is achieved by "aligning with your highest potential."

Consider these two ideas:

1. Connecting with your purpose from your heart produces great success.
2. Connecting with your purpose from your mind produces average results.

What is the difference between working from your heart and working from your mind? What does each process look like? What does each feel like?

What is it like when you wake up in the morning? Do you lie in bed dreading the day? Or are you excited to start your day?

The Importance of Purpose

Understand your purpose for waking up in the morning. The motivation for getting out of bed should be one of inspiration from your inner being, giving you full control of your goals for living life abundantly.

Purpose is the driving force behind every goal. Even bullies have goals. Every decision you make is linked to purpose. It is the cause of your existence. It is the motivation behind studying for a test or asking for help.

Acting with more Purpose

Asking for help when you need it is critical in moving closer to your purpose for living. You can only connect to your purpose based on the kind of questions you ask while on your journey. Asking questions increases your ability to be more proactive each day and will elevate your level for consciousness, allowing you to do more with more purpose.

Pay attention to the intent of your questions. If your purpose is to blame others, like your parents or teachers, it actually lowers your consciousness and moves you toward a victim mindset.

Special Note: Bullies are only attracted to victims (a reflection of themselves). Bullies are not aligned with those who are confident, strong, bold and living on purpose.

Many teens go through life feeling discouraged, thinking they do not have a purpose for living. But this is not true. Whoever you are, whatever your life experiences, wherever you live – what you do matters and there is purpose to your life. But without connecting to your purpose, there is no direction. Without direction, it feels as if what happens in your life, or to your life, is not important. Those who feel, "I am useless" have become disconnected from their purpose.

Aligning with your purpose for life is the key for living a fulfilled and happy life. By being aware of your motivations at the beginning of your day, you can start this alignment process. Each day, pay more attention to your desire to add value to this world. This is a good time to check the questions below.

"Purpose" Questions to Ponder:

1. What is a simple and remarkable way to add more value to your family, your community and yourself?
2. What would you do if you had the wisdom to improve the world?
3. What will it take to quickly train yourself to increase your capacity to share more of your skills and talents?
4. What if you had all the money in the world, who would you help and why?
5. If you had access to unlimited amounts of time, where would you invest it?

Solution

Giving, growing and being balanced are the top three essentials for developing a healthy purpose for living. Living with passion, intention and motivation are foundational in living a life that is fulfilled.

Your purpose in life is to give. Giving of your talents, your skills, your dreams, your love, your hope, your patience, your kindness, your peace, your generosity, your understanding, your knowledge and your light. The list is endless as to what you can give to yourself and others.

Your purpose in life is to grow. Grow in character, leadership, knowledge, wisdom, vision, success, self-control, determination, emotional power, kindness, integrity, and in caring for yourself and others.

Your purpose in life is to move toward balance. Balance your time, day, projects, relationships, social activities, phone time, rest, exercise, fun and relaxation time. Internal and external balances are critical to your success. It is foundational in generating enough energy for yourself and others. Understanding your purpose for living is a skill that you can build upon forever.

Quotes

"Our prime purpose in this life is to help others. And if you can't help them, at least don't hurt them."
~Dalai Lama

"Efforts and courage are not enough without purpose and direction."
~John F. Kennedy

"There is a plan and a purpose, a value to every life, no matter what its location, age, gender or disability."
~ Sharron Angle

"Any idea, plan or thought may be placed in the mind through repetition of thought."
~Napoleon Hill

Write out a sentence about how your presence will make a difference in your home, school and community within the next twelve months. Be very specific for each month.

January_____

February_____

March_____

April_____

May_____

June_____

July_____

August_____

September_____

October_____

November_____

December_____

Journal

For me, living with purpose is....

Understanding my purpose will....

Yvonne Brooks and Stephanie R. Bien, LMFT, LPCC

TIP #3

What Others Say Can Hurt You...If You Believe It!

The Truth about Opinions

The opinion you have about who you are as person can either increase your happiness or make you feel badly about yourself. Your opinion is not a fact. It is not reality. Your opinion belongs only to you. So then, what is your "opinion"?

Your opinion is a set of mutually supportive thoughts and feelings that you choose to review over and over using your mind.

What you are convinced is true, only for you because of your experiences. What others say can hurt you only if you keep reviewing the same negative and fearful thoughts over and over about who you believe you are as a person.

The Reality...

No one has the power to hurt you without your permission. Believe it or not, if someone bullies you, your thoughts have given permission to be bullied. Choosing to allow negative thoughts instead of positive thoughts to take control of your mind is giving every bully permission to treat you how you feel you can be treated. Imagine that it's as if your feelings about yourself are emitted into the atmosphere and people pick up on them.

If you feel badly about yourself, you have bought into a lie. Are you rehearsing negative thoughts about being a victim? If so, you are allowing negative thoughts to dictate who you are. If you believe those lies that make you feel badly about yourself, and if you believe that everyone is out to hurt you, it will actually bring those experiences closer to you.

When you know your truth, when you believe in who you are, you will feel good from the inside.

There will always be negative influences trying to tell you who you should be. Believing in who you are will deflect those negative inputs.

Become aware of your confidence, your joy, your strengths, your beauty, your light, your skills and your talents. Align with the value you bring to this world.

"What Others Say" Questions to Ponder:

1. What if I was content with myself?
2. What if I had authentic friendships?
3. What if I listened more and withheld judgment of others?
4. What if my relationships were more about the other person's point of view, not just mine?
5. What if I was great at managing my own life?

How to...

Rehearsing your strengths more than your weaknesses is a very powerful way to set the standards high. You have more than enough light to share with this world. Believing this statement is key to your survival.

You have the power to choose the thoughts you will honor. Make the commitment to practice believing more about your strengths and less about your faults. I dare you!

Solution

Believing more positive thoughts about who you are instead of negative thoughts is experienced on two levels. One is ignorance and the other is free choice.

The most dangerous of these two is free choice. Every time a negative thought arises you have a choice to receive it as truth or reject it as a lie. No one can make that choice for you.

Ignorance is a lot different because your level of awareness was inactive about making healthy choices. Not knowing also comes with a consequence until you ask questions to bring you into awareness of the beauty that lives in you.

It is impossible to receive an answer to a question you've never asked. To know what it will take to feel more valuable you must first ask that question to yourself or to someone who already values him/herself.

You are reading this book because you have a desire to learn how to protect yourself from bullies or how to help someone else with the issue.

It is imperative that you ask questions to increase your self-worth so that your life can be flooded with the answers. Asking negative questions about your life, your day, your family, your world will only flood your life with negative answers.

Take the time to allow a positive thought about yourself to come into your mind daily. Build a database of thoughts, emotions and pictures that make you feel good about your life. Choose to take full responsibility about believing in your abilities to give light to your family, your community and the world. Share your best self with others everyday and the same will return to you.

Quotes

"Believe that life is worth living and your belief
will help create the fact."
~William James

"Faith is to believe what you do not see;
the reward of this faith is to see what you believe."
~Saint Augustine

"Don't limit yourself. Many people limit themselves
to what they think they can do. You can go as far as your mind
lets you. What you believe, remember, you can achieve."
~Mary Kay Ash

"The future belongs to those who believe in
the beauty of their dreams."
~Eleanor Roosevelt

Yvonne Brooks and Stephanie R. Bien, LMFT, LPCC

Practice

Please think about the questions below, and then write the answers. This will give you insights and possibly a new perspective to seeing others and yourself.

What opinions do you have of yourself?

    1. _____

    2. _____

    3. _____

What stories do you tell yourself?

    1. _____

    2. _____

    3. _____

How can you replace those lies with new positive truths?

    1. _____

    2. _____

    3. _____

Believing in myself is....

A positive story about me is...

Yvonne Brooks and Stephanie R. Bien, LMFT, LPCC

TIP #4

Looking Deeper Into The Soul And Understanding Others... The Bully, The Victim And The Girl Next Door

I know that it's difficult to believe sometimes, but we are all innately good (even if the behavior isn't always good).

We live with reactions of either love or fear. Feelings of insecurity can scare us and we can feel fearful that we may be "found out." We also live in fear when we judge ourselves.

Fear doesn't allow us to be our best self. Fear makes us hide, protect ourselves, lash out and push others away from us. The one that hides can become or look like the victim, the one who lashes out can appear to be the bully.

Can I tell you a secret? We all have insecurities. We can all appear to be a victim or a bully at times - this is being human. When I learned this, it was such a relief. I could release the fear and love myself and others for being who they are. It's about acceptance. We want to be accepted for who we are so we can start by accepting ourselves and then others.

A teen boy told me of an experiment he once did. He went into a market and decided to see what happened when he was quiet and kept to himself. People ignored him, looked away and he started looking down and feeling awkward. After 10 minutes, he decided to see what would happen if he was open and kind to others. He saw that if he smiled, others smiled back. If he looked up and walked with a lightness, others were open in return. It was his fun experiment and what he realized was that he can make a difference in his environment... and so can you.

"Deeper Understanding" Questions to Ponder:

1. If you saw the good in everyone, how would this change your relationships?
2. What would happen if you were accepting of others' differences?
3. What if you felt accepted by others?
4. What if you didn't have to hide or feel ashamed about anything?
5. How would the world be different if everyone was accepted?

Solution

Let's look deeper at what's going on with all of these people: The victim, the bully, and "the girl next door." Realize that the bully is a bully because he is afraid – yes! He's afraid! What is the brainiac fearful about? And the shy girl? You? Me?

Some common fears include the fear of looking different, the fear of making a mistake and the fear of being judged. There are many other common fears that we all experience.

We can replace this fear with compassion for ourselves and others: what's going on with that person and/or me? We don't always know what's happening in their life. They have just gotten a 'D' on a test, or they've lost their best friend, or their parents are fighting at home, or they're accused of something they didn't do - the possibilities are endless. Be caring, show understanding, be compassionate and spread love and joy. Give others the benefit of the doubt. Usually what others do has nothing to do with us. They may push a person, yet they're really upset with themselves and not know how to handle that feeling.

As you read and do the exercises, you will see how to change this fear and negativity that you can feel and turn it around to make it positive and to be understanding of those around you.

Quotes

"Let us always meet each other with a smile,
for the smile is the beginning of love."
~Mother Teresa

"Love doesn't make the world go 'round.
Love is what makes the ride worthwhile."
~Franklin P. Jones

"Where there is love, there is life."
~Mahatma Gandhi

"I realized that bullying never has to do with you.
It's the bully who's insecure."
~Shay Mitchell

"If we're destroying our trees and destroying our environment
and hurting animals and hurting one another and all that stuff,
there's got to be a very powerful energy to fight that. I think we
need more love in the world. We need more kindness,
more compassion, more joy, more laughter.
I definitely want to contribute to that."
~Ellen DeGeneres

"Love and compassion are necessities, not luxuries.
Without them humanity cannot survive."
~Dalai Lama

Practice

Please think about the questions below, and then write the answers. This will give you insights and possibly a new perspective to seeing others and yourself.

I. Think of your day and find 3 situations when you felt hurt by someone's actions. Looking deeper to see if it's actually coming from their fear.

    1.

    2.

    3.

II. Think of today, or the past week, and find 3 situations that went well because of kindness, love and compassion.

    1.

    2.

    3.

III. Think of 3 situations in which you felt fearful. What kinds of decisions were you making because of the fear? Would your actions have been different if you were compassionate with yourself?

1.

2.

3.

Yvonne Brooks and Stephanie R. Bien, LMFT, LPCC

Journal

1. When I'm fearful, I may act in an aggressive way, like the time when...

2. Pick one type of person: a bully, a victim, a mean girl, etc. who did something that bothered you and write what happened and what might've been going on for them.

TIP #5

Holding Onto Anger Leads To Unhappiness

I read a book by Marshall Rosenberg called, "The Surprising Purpose of Anger." It was brilliant. It said that angry feelings are a signal that something isn't feeling right. Listen to the indication and ask yourself, "What's bothering me?" or "What's not feeling right?" Usually you will realize that something said or done isn't sitting well with you.

The Anger Iceberg Theory

The "Anger Iceberg" theory, taught by Gordon Training International and designed by Dr. Thomas Gordon, says the anger that we show is the tip, the outward view, and that underneath are other feelings like hurt, sadness, disappointment, and frustration, that is the true feelings. Why is the anger there? The anger protects me and keeps me from others. It closes me off and grows bigger and bigger inside me. It makes me feel heavy and explosive. If it stays inside then it only hurts me and keeps me from being heard or getting my needs met.

We have every right to feel upset. As Marshall Rosenberg says, "It's a signal that someone's actions don't sit well with us." If we can open up and look underneath the water below the surface of the ice, we can understand why that doesn't feel right. We can become aware of the feelings "below the surface" and then express these feelings to the person. Usually by communicating, the other will see why their behavior has affected you and ease off. The most important thing is that we now have "gotten it off our chest" by releasing it. What a relief! The weight has been lifted.

The Bully holds onto the anger and explodes it at others. The victim often holds onto the anger and allows it to hurt them inside. Neither seems to get what they want.

What do we all want?

We all want connections with others that are deep and filled with care and love. We are put here on this earth to live in peace and harmony, to stand side by side, have meaningful interactions with others and make a difference in the world by being here.

By being here on earth I wish you lightness, happiness and peace - not darkness, anger and distress.

"Feeling" Questions to Ponder:

1. How would friendships change if people would express their underlying feelings?
2. What would change if you saw others' feelings behind their anger?
3. How can you stop yourself when someone is angry at you, and not react to them?
4. What would the world look like if there was no more anger?
5. How can you make a difference in your community?

Solutions

As we see above, holding onto anger is not the answer. So what is? Expressing the anger isn't always the most helpful solution either. When we tell another person that we are angry with them, we are indirectly telling the other that they are wrong. We call that a "you" message which means that they hear blame coming their way and put up a wall to block it and then may lash back and defend themselves. This cycle prevents productive conflict resolution.

Here is another idea that can lead to a solution and a productive, peaceful interaction. Remember we spoke of the iceberg theory? This shows the anger on the surface but there are other feelings deep down like pain, sadness, frustration, confusion, fear, and embarrassment. Expressing these feelings with an "I" message like, "I felt hurt when others were invited to the birthday party and I wasn't." By doing this you show a softer, more vulnerable side of yourself and the other can open up (rather than be defensive) and hear you. (Dr. Thomas Gordon)

If speaking to another person isn't possible for some reason, there are other ways to release the anger.

★Write a cathartic letter that won't be sent if you don't want to,

- Yell into a pillow
- Walk or run around the block

- Punch a punching bag
- Talk to a friend or adult to get it off your chest

... and I bet you can come up with many more ideas that would work also. Find what works for you!

Quotes

"If another can easily anger you, it is because you are off balance with yourself."
~Unknown

"Everyday we have plenty of opportunities to get angry, stressed or offended but what you're doing when you indulge these negative emotions is giving something outside yourself power over your happiness. You can choose to not let little things upset you."
~Joel Osteen

"Holding on to anger is like grasping a hot coal with the intent of throwing it at someone else; you are the one who gets burned."
~Buddha

"Whatever is begun in anger ends in shame."
~Benjamin Franklin

"When you judge another, you do not define them, you define you."
~Wayne Dyer

"Forgive people in your life, even those who are not sorry for their actions. Holding on to anger only hurts you, not them."
~Unknown

Practice

List 3 situations that you have recently felt angry about. Using the Iceberg Theory, check off the underlying feelings you had at the time about these situations...

1. _____

        ____ fear

        ____ sadness

        ____ embarrassment

        ____ pain

        ____ frustration

        ____ other

2. _____

        ____ fear

        ____ sadness

        ____ embarrassment

        ____ hurt

        ____ frustration

        ____ other

3. _____

        ____ fear

        ____ sadness

        ____ embarrassment

Yvonne Brooks and Stephanie R. Bien, LMFT, LPCC

_____ hurt
_____ frustration
_____ other

★ *Change a blaming "you" message to an "I" message by using the P.E.T. model.*

I feel a._____ when b._____ because c._____

    a. is the feeling you have about the behavior

    b. the behavior – make sure it's something you see or hear rather than a judgment. For example, Bossy is a judgment but telling me what to do every morning and every night is a behavior that you can hear.

    c. is a concrete, tangible effect – that is how the behavior affects you – a loss of time, money or energy. Example: extra time and energy having conversations about this.

    So, if a "you" message is "You always bug me about schoolwork. Get off my back!"

    Then an "I" message would be: "I feel (a) sad and distrusted when (b) I'm asked if I'm done with my schoolwork because (c) it takes away study time and energy to explain it to you."

I feel _____ when _____ because then

_____.

I feel _____ when _____ because then

_____.

★Taken from Effectiveness Training, Dr. Thomas Gordon

When I hold in my anger, I ...

I noticed that when I'm angry, I have trouble relating to the person I'm upset with and I...

TIP #6

Have Spirituality In Your Life…

I know that each and every one of you is different.

You've been brought up with your own religion and beliefs. Our homes are all unique. I have found that my life has been enhanced by spirituality.

What is spirituality? I had to Google it because the concept isn't concrete. One definition is, "Spirituality may refer to almost any kind of meaningful activity." Other definitions suggest a connection to something bigger than ourselves, G-d, light, goodness, universality, a higher power…the list continues. Take a moment to think of your definition of spirituality…

Now, I'll share one teen girl's story:

"I was adopted at 14 months old. My mom was a single mother and was very religious. We went to church weekly and I went to Sunday school. As I got older, I attended the kids activity club with other middle schoolers. As I got older, I started to rebel against my mom. I was angry that I had no dad, that I was adopted and felt my mom always told me what to do. I stopped going to church and didn't want to have anything to do with religion. In high school I started hanging out with kids who smoked a lot so I went along with them. My grades started dropping and I felt very unproductive. School had always been important to me. I had goals since I was in 4th grade to become a Veterinarian. Now this wasn't looking so good. One day, my mom and I were running errands and we ran into the director of the Sunday school. She asked if I wanted to work as a teacher's assistant at Sunday school and that I'd be paid. Well, I did need money...so I said "OK". This moment changed my life. I liked the work so much and they liked me, so they asked if I could help out in the kids activity club during the week. I agreed to that as well. I was at church and running into my old friends. We started making plans and my grades started to improve. I no longer was smoking, drinking or hanging out with those other friends and I felt different... back to myself. I realized that the day I ran into the director was so life changing–it was life saving. I was guided by my higher power to be in the right place at the right time."

The most important lesson is that life works so much smoother when connected to the universe. We are never alone. Be grateful for even the smallest things - like the sunshine, a tree with leaves changing their colors, a beautiful butterfly, an enormous mountain, and the voluminous ocean that seems to have its own rhythm. With all of this beauty there must be something greater than man alone. Creation is amazing and miraculous.

Where in this tip is the bully? I noticed that it's not here at all. Maybe because when there's spirituality, being hurt or hurting others doesn't exist. Integrity and ethics prevail.

All that I ask is that you be open to the idea and test it out.

Search and find questions and answers to help you develop your own beliefs.

"Spirituality" Questions to Ponder:

1. What makes up your spirituality?
2. What does it mean to be a good person?
3. What is your life purpose?
4. What is the meaning of life?
5. Do things happen for a reason?

Solution

Ask people that you respect. Ask those that seem happy and content with their life. Do some reading or search on the Internet. Many of the quotes that we used in this book are people who have an understanding of their own spirituality so you may want to read more of their works. Another way that I get in touch with my spirituality is by sitting quietly and meditating, listening to nature or taking a walk. Each time I come across a bird soaring in the sky, a bird chirping, a child laughing gleefully, I am in amazement and wonderment.

A belief in a Higher Power allows us to trust and let go. We don't have full control of our lives or our world. We can let go of some of that burden we may feel and carry. As hard as we try to make our lives a certain way, have you noticed that forcing it never works? We need to do the footwork and put in our best effort, but then we can sit back and see what happens. Trust in nature and the flow of the universe.

Quotes

"I believe God is managing affairs and that He doesn't need any advice from me. With God in charge, I believe everything will work out for the best in the end. So what is there to worry about?"
~ Henry Ford

"God writes the Gospel not in the Bible alone, but also on trees, and in the flowers and clouds and stars."
~Martin Luther

"In order to experience everyday spirituality, we need to remember that we are spiritual beings spending some time in a human body."
~Barbara de Angelis

"The best remedy for those who are afraid, lonely or unhappy is to go outside, somewhere where they can be quiet, alone with the heavens, nature and God. Because only then does one feel that all is as it should be."
~Anne Frank

"When the solution is simple, God is answering."
~Albert Einstein

"Spirituality is meant to take us beyond our tribal identity into a domain of awareness that is more universal."
~Deepak Chopra

Please think about the questions below, and then write the answers. This will give you insights and possibly a new perspective to seeing others and yourself.

1. Look around and find 3 objects that you see to be a sign of spirituality:

    1.

    2.

    3.

2. Name a time that something happened and you were completely and happily surprised. It could be a coincidence, like a friend showing up when you needed them most, glancing up and seeing the place you were looking for right in front of you, or getting a call from someone that you were just thinking about...

(Albert Einstein once wrote, "Coincidence is God's way of remaining anonymous.")

Journal

What can I do that would help me become a spiritual person?

The benefits of having spirituality in my life is...

TIP #7

By Giving to Others, You Receive As Well

There is an ancient saying, "you reap what you sow." The meaning of this saying is that as you are able to give more patience, more kindness, and more support to others, you will receive the same exact proportion to what you sowed, nothing more and nothing less.

Your results will always be yours and not another person's. If you do not like the results you currently have, it's time to practice giving that which you desire to receive.

Receiving to give is the ultimate state of being where bullies will never be found. You see, bullies are only interested in receiving for themselves. The emptiness bullies feel causes them to be in constant want of what other people have. But their victimizations cannot fix their low self-worth.

True fulfillment comes through the habit of receiving to give. The more you receive, the more de-cluttering needs to take place.

The desire to have people respect you requires that you first receive respect for yourself then you can respect others. Disrespect is a negative state of mind. It's a mind focused on dark thoughts (receiving only).

Respect can never be earned. Respect is a result of doing internal work. It's investing time monitoring every negative thought that tries to influence your mind. Respect is being vigilant on doing good deeds to others because that is exactly what the payoff will be in return to you.

Giving respect to your parents, your teachers, your friends and to strangers will generate the exact same level of respect not necessarily from those you give it to, but by those whom have already achieved a level of respect for themselves and others.

Receiving for the sake of giving to others is the highest form of fulfillment. It is the only way to set in motion a series of never ending events that cause you to receive as well.

"Giving to Others" Questions to Ponder:

1. What if I gave to others more than I take?
2. What if I gave more peace to the world?
3. What if I created a weekly giving plan?
4. What if my life was measured by my giving?
5. What if my receiving capacity reflected my giving level?

Solution

The places you go and the people whom you connect, bring a gift. A gift symbolizes your inner desire to receive the same. The gift could be a smile, forgiveness, patience or a prayer that brings peace to their lives.

Position yourself to gratefully receive all that is available for you to receive daily. Think about the gifts you would like to give to your parents, your siblings, your friends, and your neighbors.

There are endless opportunities each day for you to practice receiving so you can continue the fulfillment that comes with giving.

Make a commitment to keep joy circulating in your life by giving and receiving life's precious gifts of laughter, happiness and tranquility. Each time someone enters your atmosphere, silently wish them gifts of love, peace and joy. Your whole life will change for the better with this simple exercise.

Yvonne Brooks and Stephanie R. Bien, LMFT, LPCC

Quotes

"Giving opens the way for receiving."
~Florence Scovel Shinn

"Asking is the beginning of receiving. Make sure you don't go to the ocean with a teaspoon. At least take a bucket so the kids won't laugh at you."
~Jim Rohn

"If you are giving love and not receiving it, you are not in the right relationship. If you are receiving it and not giving it, then you are taking advantage of the other person."
~Patti Stanger

"God never gives someone a gift they are not capable of receiving. If he gives us the gift of Christmas, it is because we all have the ability to understand and receive it."
~Pope Francis

Create a list of gifts you will commit to sharing with others this week.

Parents

_____

_____

Teachers

_____

_____

Friends

_____

_____

Neighbors

_____

_____

Classmates

_____

_____

Strangers

_____

_____

Yvonne Brooks and Stephanie R. Bien, LMFT, LPCC

Journal

I desire to share...

A time I received something that made me happy was when.....

TIP #8

Positive Energy Brings About More Positive Energy

Everything that affects your life is connected to energy. Your thoughts, how you feel, the words you speak, the decisions you make, the clothing you wear and especially the music you listen to, all carry their own energy.

Positive energy is associated with the things you think and do that bring vitality, good health, peace of mind, joy, healing, gratitude, and love directly back to you.

Energy is attracted to vibration. Positive energy can only vibrate itself. To vibrate someone in your atmosphere that treats you with respect, honor and love, you would first have to practice the same vibration of respect, honor and love within yourself for it to connect with you.

When you emit positive energy through your thoughts, emotions and your vibrations, positive energy magnetically finds its way back to you.

Bullies and victims often vibrate a negative energy that matches how they feel about themselves and others. Vibrating negative energy is the main connection between the bully/victim relationship. They are like two magnets that attract each other.

Positive energy is also magnetic, and often vibrates the highest emotions for life transformation. Maintaining a focus of feeling that no matter what life throws at you, all things will work out for your good, is key.

The feeling of wellbeing is fundamental for holding onto positive energy. In this high-energy atmosphere no harm will ever come to you.

When you're at the level of vibrating positive energy, it's the perfect time to study, make decisions, connect with mutually beneficial relationships, set goals, exercise, eat for fuel and much more.

Everything you will ever connect to in your life is connected to energy. Practicing positive thoughts, emotions, and vibrations will produce more positive energy for expanding happiness in your life.

"Positive Energy" Questions to Ponder:

1. What if I mastered the art of generating unlimited positive energy?
2. What if I vibrated positive energy?
3. What if I had more than enough energy to care for myself and others?
4. What if I took time out to power up when I needed it?
5. What if I was responsible with how I use my energy?

Solution

There are many ideas for vibrating positive energy in your day-to-day routine that will take your life to the highest potential. Taking the time to reflect on the following ideas is the beginning of taking control of what and whom you will attract into your life.

Commit to being the best you could be everyday.
Raise the bar on your thoughts;
Positive feelings and high vibrations should be your greatest quest.
Write out a fresh list daily of the things you
love and accept about your life.
Refuse to give your power away by allowing negative
thoughts and emotions to guide your path.
Practice thoughts that increase your joy level.
Say "NO" to feelings linked to guilt, shame, doubt and fear.
Allow inner love to be your best friend.
Let go of the desire to control how people feel about you.
Pay more attention to feeling good in each moment.
Find something good in every situation.
Allow your light to shine.

Quotes

"An attitude of positive expectation is the mark
of the superior personality."
~ *Brian Tracy*

"With everything that has happened to you, you can
either feel sorry for yourself or treat what has happened as a gift.
Everything is either an opportunity to grow or an obstacle to
keep you from growing. You get to choose."
~*Dr. Wayne W Dyer*

"Believe in yourself! Have faith in your abilities!
Without a humble but reasonable confidence in your
own powers you cannot be successful or happy."
~*Norman Vincent Peale*

"Hate. It has caused a lot of problems in this world
but has not solved one yet."
~*Maya Angelou*

"Happiness is an attitude. We either make ourselves miserable,
or happy and strong. The amount of work is the same."
~*Francesca Reigler*

Practice

Please think about the questions below, and then write the answers. Pay attention to the changes that you experience.

Take a minute to send yourself positive energy. What do you feel during and after this process?

1. _____
2. _____
3. _____

De-clutter your room. How do you feel in the cleared space?

1. _____
2. _____
3. _____

Write down a list of things you have been procrastinating about. Then go do them. What are your feelings after accomplishing this assignment?

1. _____

_____

2. _____

_____

3. _____

_____

Yvonne Brooks and Stephanie R. Bien, LMFT, LPCC

Journal

Vibrating positive energy in my life looks like....

Raising the bar feels like...

TIP #9

Take A Moment To Breathe Before Reacting...

Taking a timeout before you react will spare you many regrets. Do you ever say something you don't mean or regret it even as it's coming out of your mouth? I have! We all do. There's no taking it back either. It really hurts the other person, it hurts the relationship, and it hurts our own self- image.

When people bully, this is often where it comes from. They have feelings and don't stop to think about what to do about those feelings so they lash out to hurt others so as to protect themselves.

Taking a breath gives you a moment to think about what to do with the feelings (but let's also look at options of dealing with sadness and/or painful feelings. This will be discussed in the solution section.)

So curbing your impulses lets you think of a response that will bring about positive change and maintain your relationships - whether it's with family, friends, a teacher or another person. This is a way to feel good about your response and about yourself.

Even though I've had years of practice, sometimes I can have trouble with my impulse control, so I'm working on ways of getting control. An option is "breathe" but sometimes that's not enough. I can walk away and take a timeout, and come back when I'm calmer. I can choose my words more carefully when I have time out. Sometimes I take a walk around the block, call a friend, or journal about the situation, but the important thing is to go back and finish the communication and have closure.

"Breathe" Questions to Ponder:

1. What can you do to stop yourself from reacting?
2. Who in your life seems impulsive?
3. How can words hurt?
4. Who do you know that stays calm rather than reacting?

Reacting to a situation seems to stem from a feeling, so let's address the feelings. How do we know what the feeling is? Often times we can feel it in our stomach or chest, but we can also feel it elsewhere. Then our body reacts.

If you feel your body reacting, stop! You may even try imagining a stop sign to help you pause for a moment. Counting backwards from ten can also help. Find a way to interfere with an immediate reaction to give yourself time to make a good decision of how best to respond in a calm, cool and collected way. Sometimes we aren't aware of the feeling, it just shows up and surprises us. Find signs of what happens to you before you get upset. They may be subtle like your heart beating fast or a gurgle in your stomach.

One girl I spoke with became aware that she balled up her fists when she was angry or scared. Then when she noticed this happening, she stopped and realized, "I must be upset about something." Then she was able to take a moment and breathe.

Quotes

"Never cut a tree down in the winter time. Never make a negative decision in the low time. Never make your most important decisions when you are in your worst moods. Wait. Be patient. The storm will pass. The spring will come."

~Robert H. Schuller

"I believe that a trusting attitude and a patient attitude go hand in hand. You see, when you let go and learn to trust G-d, it releases joy in your life. And when you trust G-d, you're able to be more patient. Patience is not just waiting for something… It's about how you wait, or your attitude while waiting."

~Joyce Meyer

"Music is a means of giving form to our inner feelings, without attaching them to events or objects in the world."

~George Santayana

"He who can no longer pause to wonder and stand rapt in awe, is as good as dead; his eyes are closed."

~Albert Einstein

Practice

Please think about the questions below, and then write the answers. This will give you insights and possibly a new perspective to seeing others and yourself.

1. Write 3 options of things you can do to stop yourself from reacting. This breaks the cycle.

    1.

    2.

    3.

2. Learn to identify your feelings. You can get a daily checklist of feelings and use this daily for 3 weeks to help you identify what it is that you're feeling. You can journal, use a feeling app, watch a relaxation video, learn deep breathing and watch for your personal signs – clenching jaw or fist, or going into fight mode.

Journal

I remember a time that I reacted to a feeling and then regretted it. This is what happened...

Take a situation that you regretted your response and now write what could've happened if you took time to respond...

TIP #10

Accept and Love Yourself

No one can accept and love you any more than you love yourself.

Accepting and loving yourself means being filled with inner joy, inner peace, inner love and the endless list based on what you are capable of receiving.

When your inner being (your sense of self) is filled up with the things you desire to experience in life, you will operate at your highest capacity. When your inner being is empty you feel low sense of self making you more open to developing relationships with bullies and victims.

Victims and bullies belong to the same mindset~ **fear**; therefore, the only way to prevent bullies entering your atmosphere is to stay filled up with the things you would like to experience~ **love**, NOT the things you do not want to experience.

The first step in accepting and loving yourself is to practice believing daily that you are lovable. Every part of your body, your mind, your character, your sense of humor or lack of it, everything about you is lovable.

Loving yourself should be one of the easiest goals on your daily to–do list. Being patience and kind to yourself and to others are results to look for. This will help to identify what loving yourself looks like.

If you find yourself being angry, mean, gossiping or impatient, it is a sure sign of being empty on the inside. And if you're emitting that negative vibration, guess who is now looking to connect with you? The bully.

Accepting and loving yourself takes work. Inner work will challenge you to raise the bar in asking questions to move you into a realm that is more peaceful, loving, kind and joyful.

Living in a bully-free realm means accepting and loving yourself beyond measure. It means making a commitment to emotional health and wellbeing not self-pity and blaming others for how you feel.

"Accept and Love Yourself" Questions to Ponder:

1. What decisions do you need to make so as to accept and love yourself more?
2. How does your decisions align with your values?
3. If you knew you could not fail, what would you attempt?
4. If you had unlimited resources how would you take better care of yourself?
5. What if you did not hurt anymore?

Solution

Investing time working on an image through visualization about how you see yourself is critical during the process of learning how to accept and love yourself.

Refrain from judging yourself and being critical about the way you look or how you do things. This confidence is essential for keeping bullies out of your atmosphere.

Reassure yourself that whatever hard time you are going through, it is only temporary and will not last. Keeping this in mind will put a limit on how long a negative experience will stay in your life.

Remembering the amazing things you are good at and have accomplished so far in your life will increase your value and self-worth for keeping your emotional frequency aligned.

Being grateful for the little, the big, the good and the bad in your life are ways of keeping the same temperature on your emotional response to life.

Being aware that you are responsible for how you feel and what you think brings instant healing to any and all situations that do not belong in your atmosphere.

Quotes

"Beauty is when you appreciate yourself. When you love yourself, that's when you are the most beautiful."

~ Zoe Kravitz

"Don't ever criticize yourself. Don't go around all day thinking, "I'm unattractive, I'm slow, I'm not as smart as my brother." God was not having a bad day when he made you…... If you don't love yourself in the right way, you can't love your neighbor. You can't be as good as you are supposed to be."

~ Joel Osteen

"You have to love yourself, or else you will never be able to accept compliments from anyone."

~Dean Wareham

"Don't forget to love yourself."

~Soren Kierkegaard

Visualize an image using your imagination of what you would like to see in the following areas. Write down or draw your image.

Your Body

_____

_____

Your Future

_____

_____

Your Attitude

_____

_____

Your Self-Esteem

_____

_____

Your Family

_____

_____

Your World

_____

_____

Journal

I accept and love myself when….

I can keep bullies away by…

TIP #11

Speaking Badly About Another Brings Negativity Back To You

A big part of bullying is verbal and cyberbullying. Do you know that by putting out negativity about others, you attract the darkness back to yourself?

That's right. By speaking about another, judging another, focusing on negative traits, sharing negative news or flaws of another, it will come back to you. I know this is hard because people all around us do this. They gossip. How do you stop being a part of that? Walk away or say, "I'm trying not to speak about others." It's difficult to be different but after awhile it gets easier and you will be a role model to others. You could create change and make a difference in the world. Be a leader. Lead others to lightness and create positive energy around you and your friends and loved ones. It's not just teens that do this. You have learned gossiping from family. It's passed down from generation to generation.

The problem that occurs is that if there hasn't been a time that you were talked about, there will be. It could be truth or something made up. It could be a picture or something that you're not proud of, but in any case, it feels horrible to be on the other end. How would it make you feel to be talked about?

Yvonne Brooks and Stephanie R. Bien, LMFT, LPCC

I realized that I didn't like gossip, but sometimes people would continue to tell me things, and I'd feel uncomfortable. I wasn't sure what to do about this, so I'd start to say, "Oh, I don't want to hear about someone else." If they continued I'd say, "I'm working on not gossiping and I need your help. It's hard for me." People were extremely helpful, and finally my friends didn't tell me things about others. I remember once, a friend of mine told me a secret of another friend of ours before I could stop her. A year later, I had something private to share to just a few friends and I didn't share it with that friend. I wasn't even sure why not, until I thought about it. I remembered that she told me a secret and I didn't want her talking to others about my private business, so I just didn't tell her.

Gossip, even if it seems harmless, causes problems on so many levels. This story shows the negative effects of gossip:

A very nice and friendly Starbucks owner would "spill the beans," so to speak, and talk to everyone about everybody's business. They'd meet their friends or talk on the phone in line and he knew it all. It was harmless and he was just making conversation. One Saturday, he was in the market and saw a holy man look at apples and put one in his bag and walk out. Well, the man couldn't believe the holy man stole an apple. How dishonest! And the next day he told some customers what he saw: "The holiest man in town took an apple without paying." His wife met some friends for brunch and told them. Soon, the entire town was talking about the dishonest man. Someone came to the holy man confronting him about this. He asked where he'd heard that and went to Starbucks owner. He explained that he doesn't use money on Saturday so he had paid the market the day before but now everyone thinks he's a thief. His reputation was destroyed and he lost face in the community. The holy man asked the Starbucks owner to come to his office the next day and to bring a feather pillow. Feeling badly, the owner said, "Sure, anything." The owner climbed the three flights of stairs and knocked on the man's office door. Expecting him, he opened the door. Again, the nice and friendly Starbucks owner apologized and told him how sorry he was and asked what he could do to make it up to him. The holy man said, "Take this pillow and cut it open, now go on the balcony and shake all the feathers out." The owner did what he was told. When he stepped back in the room, the wise, holy man said, "Now go bring me back every last feather." The owner said, "I can't, they spread far and wide in the breeze." The holy man said, "Exactly, you can not take back the rumor you spread. You don't know where it all went."

This demonstrates the deep roots that a negative or untrue statement can do to affect a person's reputation and their life.

"Gossip" Questions to Ponder:

1. How can you train yourself to speak positively?
2. What do you think about others who gossip?
3. Think about what difference you can make by sharing this with one friend?
4. What would life be like if there wasn't any gossiping?
5. How would you bring positivity into your environment?

Solution

You might say, "Everyone at my school does this," and you'd be right that most do share gossip. The problem with gossiping is how you feel when you speak negatively about others. You don't feel good. This kind of communication lowers your vibration. You also wouldn't feel good if others spread rumors about you. Just like the Starbucks owner learned, "You can't take it back once it's out there." Best options are to just talk about yourself. Share yourself with your friends. This will create a deeper connection with your friends. If you don't trust your friends not to spread rumors about you or share something negative, then these are not the people that you want to spend time with.

If someone hurts you, rather than gossiping to others about it, you can directly work it out with the person. Go to them and use I-messages like the ones we learned in tip #5. Express your feelings and work things out with a resolution that you're both comfortable with. Both take responsibility for your part in the situation and apologize. If this is too difficult or you need help, you can ask a parent, counselor, therapist or mentor to help you work out some hard feelings you have with another.

Quotes

"Be impeccable with your word. Speak with integrity. Say only what you mean. Avoid using the word to speak against yourself or to gossip about others. Use the power of your word in the direction of truth and love."

~Miguel Angel Ruiz

"Gossip can be entertaining occasionally. I've heard the most fascinating thing about myself I never knew."

~Vanna Borita

"I have been effected by gossip and I know people who have been too. I've seen marriages destroyed by gossip. It is cruel. At the end of the day, all that matters is: Do you love what you see when you look in the mirror? That is it, baby."

~Jada Pinkett Smith

"Live in such a way that you would not be ashamed to sell your parrot to the town gossip."

~Will Rogers

Practice

Please think about and write the answers below. This will give you insights and possibly a new perspective to seeing others and yourself.

A time when people found out something that I didn't want known.

_____

_____

_____

How I felt when I found out.

_____

_____

_____

Journal

Things I can do when I want to gossip are...

Things I can do when others are telling me something about someone else...

 Yvonne Brooks and Stephanie R. Bien, LMFT, LPCC

TIP #12

Worry Only Wastes Time And Energy

I think we know that worrying is a waste of our time and energy, but we may not always be aware when it is happening. Most importantly, we need to know how to do something about it.

We worry, then we beat ourselves up for worrying, but we continue to worry anyways. When we beat ourselves up, we accept self-bullying and become used to this harsh treatment. We may even feel it's ok. We become used to this negativity and self-criticism allowing others the open door to treat us poorly and be critical of us also.

We also see others worrying. It could be parents, adults and friends. This appears in many forms. Parents often express their worry related to their children by trying to take control. They may be worried and feel out of control, so to remedy the worry, they put up protective walls around you. As you know, it doesn't feel good to be caged in and it doesn't work. You just want to break away.

When other adults in your life worry, it may look like adulthood is a burden. There are so many problems and pressures to be an adult. The future doesn't seem like a place that we want to rush to get to. This worry is not necessary, it's just that these adults have not learned the lesson or rule about worry. You may be able to teach them because below you will find a way to let go of worry, to be free and to live life.

Your friends likely worry about things like tests, grades, the future and relationships. All the worry in the world will not solve these concerns. It just zaps time and energy, creating more worry. It's a vicious cycle and a time pit.

Another way people may deal with their worry is by numbing it out. There are many ways to numb your brain and temporarily stop the worry. Sometimes it's with drugs, alcohol, food, games, work — anything that's excessive. The problem with these excessive distractions is that they hurt you physically and emotionally, making you feel badly about yourself — and, ironically, the thing you were worried about is still there! This type of hurting yourself is another invitation for others to bully or hurt you.

"Worry" Questions to Ponder:

1. What would you do with your extra time and energy if you weren't worrying?
2. How would your self esteem change if you were trusting of yourself?
3. How does worrying help you?
4. How would your life change without worry?
5. What can you replace worry with?

Solution

Worrying about anything from the past is a complete waste of time. The past is over and you aren't able to change it. Find a way of completing what happened, come clean and express your feelings. Apologize for your part and when you feel complete and have gone to everyone that was involved, "let it go".

Worrying about the future zaps you of energy to come up with solutions. If you lose sleep over worry, it takes away precious sleep time where you should rejuvenate your body, mind and soul. If you're not sleeping, you're exhausted and probably seeing the problem as even bigger than it may be. Instead, brainstorm ideas and then look for ways to find answers. Sit quietly with yourself and think of what would be helpful. Ask trustworthy adults like a parent, a counselor, a teacher, a grandparent, an aunt, an uncle or a religious leader for assistance. Make sure that they help you look for options, not just tell you what to do.

The bottom line – Don't waste time worrying. Take action and stay open to finding a solution to your concern. Stay in the present.

Quotes

"I believe G-d is managing affairs and that he doesn't need any advice from me. With G-d in charge, I believe everything will work out for the best in the end. So what is there to worry about."

~Henry Ford

"It is not the end of the physical body that should worry us. Rather, our concern must be to live while we're alive - to release our inner selves from the spiritual death that comes with living behind a facade designed to conform to external definitions of who and what we are."

~Elizabeth Kubler-Ross

"Our fatigue is often caused not by work, but by worry, frustration and resentment."

~Dale Carnegie

"A day of worry is more exhausting than a week of work."

~John Lubbock

"I try to keep it real. I don't have time to worry about what I'm projecting to the world. I'm just busy being myself".

~Demi Lovato

"We humans have lost the wisdom of genuinely resting and relaxing. We worry too much. We don't allow our bodies to heal, and we don't allow our minds and hearts to heal".

~Thich Nhat Hanh

Practice

Please think about the questions below, and then write the answers. This will give you insights and possibly a new perspective to seeing others and yourself.

1. Take a worry/regret from the past and make amends. Write down the people involved and have a resolution with each. Apologize for your part.

<u>People</u>   <u>Resolution</u>

_____   _____

_____   _____

_____   _____

Conclusion – What I did, what helped, how I felt:

_____

_____

_____

_____

2. Think of a worry that you have. Brainstorm ideas to solve your worry. Ask for help with your brainstorming. Everyone is a teacher, so ask for suggestions to add to your list – you may not use them but thank all those who shared with you.

Brainstorming

1.

2.

3.

4.

5.

6.

7.

8.

9.

10.

Journal

To live in the present, worry free, I can...

If I didn't worry, I'd have more time to....

TIP #13

Take Quiet Time Daily, Even if it's Only Five Minutes

Taking quiet time daily to align your mind to a peaceful state is the most powerful way to give your soul a holiday and experience mental and emotional freedom.

Lack of down time increases your negative stress level, making it easier to fall victim to negative habits. Once your emotional frequency is lowered, your chance of effectiveness is lowered.

Each day, your new goal is to bring calmness into your life. Calmness is power – power over negative thoughts, emotions and fears. Calmness is the greatest antidote for negative thoughts, negative emotions, low self-esteem, irritation and fear.

Allowing yourself to have five minutes of quiet time can make a big difference in your quality of life. Giving yourself quiet time helps you prepare for a big test, it helps you negotiate with your parents if they are asking too much of you, and it helps you give time or energy to a friend who may need your support. If you don't give yourself time to rest, you won't have reserves for giving to anyone – including yourself!

Yvonne Brooks and Stephanie R. Bien, LMFT, LPCC

Life is about how you handle it, not what is happening to you. Five minutes of "me time" can make all the difference in how you respond to stressful situations, things and people. Effectiveness not busyness is the name of the game.

The ability to cope and deal with life no matter the good or bad comes from taking quiet time to de-clutter every thought in your mind that has a plan to disturb your wellbeing.

Your overall wellbeing is essential in dealing with bullies. Feeling strong, joyful, confident and fulfilled are the highest forms of protection against bullies who cannot stand to be in an atmosphere of calmness.

Taking quiet time is a gift you choose to receive so as to give to those situations and people waiting to give you the opportunity for expanding your effectiveness. It is setting the standard of how you would like to feel in-control and not be controlled (by things, situations or people).

"Quiet Time" Questions to Ponder:

1. What if you had control of your time?
2. What could you do to enjoy regular quiet time?
3. What kind of character would you need to develop so as to value quiet time?
4. How will you cherish your time more?
5. What will it take for you to take responsibility for the time you give away to disappointments, distractions, anxiety and worry?

Solution

Take Quiet Time

At all costs protect yourself by taking quiet time. Smell the roses, enjoy the beach, go for a hike or take yourself on a picnic. Recognize and appreciate the value you bring to this world.

Use quiet time as a priority for centering your mind in preparation for each day. Starting your day in your power zone is the most empowering idea for drawing the line between yourself and bullies.

Say No!

Saying "No" to things that lower your energy is a must for maintaining your inner power. Filling up with inner energy is essential for increasing your effectiveness at home, at school, with your friends and within the community. Saying "No" to too many activities, assignments, social outings, entertainment, or social media time will leave you with plenty of energy to be used for increasing your inner power.

Spend Time By Yourself

Solitude can bring about an opportunity for freedom in your mind. It is in solitude that you face your darkest thoughts. The willingness to allow alone time and quietness to counsel your mind inspirationally is the most powerful technique by far to expand your effectiveness in every area of your life.

Ask For Help

Wise teenagers usually ask lots of questions. Questions are your greatest allies. The power of a question can take you from one dimension of thought to several dimensions in receiving answers based on how proactive your questions are. Becoming a master of taking full responsibility in controlling how you feel and think will always be linked to the questions you are asking, conscious or unconscious. Being aware (conscious of your questions) will bring more possibilities.

Quotes

"We need quiet time to examine our lives openly and honestly. Spending quiet time alone gives your mind an opportunity to renew itself and create order."

~*Susan L Taylor*

"Solitude is very different from a "time-out' from our busy lives. Solitude is the very ground from which community grows. Whenever we pray alone, study, read, write or simply just spend quiet time away from the places we interact with each other directly, we are potentially opened for a deeper intimacy with each other."

~*Henri Nouwen*

"Finding some quiet time in your life I think is hugely important."

~*Mariel Hemingway*

"It's important to have quiet time and isolation."

~*John Burnside*

Practice

Please think about the questions below, and then write the answers. This will give you insights and possibly a new perspective to seeing others and yourself.

Start your day with gratitude (Allow 5 minutes). Write down a list of things you are grateful for and would like to experience again.

1. _____

2. _____

3. _____

4. _____

5. _____

Taking quiet time for myself makes me feel....

The issue that I have is.... and I can ask who for help with this...

TIP#14

Pay Attention All Around You. Listen To Everyone - Teachers Come In All Sizes And Forms.

When I'm aware, I see signs all around me. I just need a reminder.

We can learn from a baby who cries when they're expressing a need in the only way they can. We can also learn from a bird who wildly flaps its wings to gain momentum but soon glides, gently enjoying the soar.

For me, I get busy in the day-to-day routine and don't pay attention to what's going on outside myself, but when I do, I really slow down and learn by the teachers around me. It fills my life with purpose and joy.

How is this related to bullying?

Why would someone lash out? Let's learn from what the bullying behavior is telling us. It says, "I'm hurt. I don't feel good about myself. and I feel lesser than." The reactions to these feelings are…"I'm going to put another person down to lift myself up and give me some power because I feel powerless." That person is my teacher. I start to understand what a person's behavior means. He/she has taught us about human nature. We learn that when we feel badly, we need to find other ways to help us feel better.

Lessons are around us. We just need to pay attention to the lessons. Even though I am an adult I learn from children, adults, animals, flowers, and people – people I may like and people I may not like. I learn how I want to be and how not to be. To learn from these "teachers" I just need to stay open and aware of the messages that come my way.

"Teacher" Questions to Ponder:

1. What would you do with more wisdom?
2. Who have you learned from and were surprised about where that came from?
3. When looking at nature, what can you learn?
4. What do you observe when you see young children?
5. How can people learn from you?

Solution

When I can see that everyone is my teacher, and that all that happens are lessons for me to grow – even if it's painful – I trust the universe that this is exactly what I need at this time. The reminder to myself that "I can learn from this" takes away my fear of what might happen.

Let's try to see the event or person in a positive light. This shift can open our minds and our eyes to the "good" of the situation, the "growth" of the moment, and the "opportunity" to see an area of ourselves that needs to be tweaked a bit. We have the chance to learn and grow everyday for the rest of our lives. This keeps us passionate about life, aware of the present moment, and in search of expansion (being our best selves).

Fulfillment comes from internalizing the positive, the new, and working towards healing the hurt or pain. We all have the ability to transform the hurts by acknowledging the awareness and lesson that is underlying the pain. Finding the positive spin of the underlying message can heal the hurt. You have the power. By taking the good, you transform the negative. This enlightens you and you will no longer react to the negative. The Bully loses the power to hurt and just walks away. They no longer have the power over you, they become powerless. You also can quietly thank them for teaching you the lesson that you needed. Their internal pain has been lifted as well – they aren't seen as "bad" anymore (at least by you) and this brings healing to them. You have had the chance now to give of yourself to them. You've done a good deed, an act of kindness, and may have made a difference to another person who could have been the next victim.

"In school, you're taught a lesson and then given a test. In life, you're given a test that teaches you a lesson."

~Tom Bodett

"I truly believe that everything that we do and everyone that we meet is out in our path for a purpose. There are no accidents; we are all teachers – if we're willing to pay attention to the lessons we learn, trust our positive instincts and not be afraid to take risks or wait for some miracle to come knocking at our door."

~Marla Gibbs

"It's fine to celebrate success but it is more important to heed the lessons of failure."

~Bill Gates

"One of the lessons that I grew up with was to always stay true to yourself and never let what somebody else says distract you from your goals. And so when I hear about negative and false attacks I really don't invest any energy in them because I know who I am."

~Michelle Obama

Practice

Please think about the questions below, and then write the answers. This will give you insights and possibly a new perspective.

Spend the next 2 hours paying attention to all that is going on around you and find 3 lessons. Jot them down.

1.

2.

3.

Now see these lessons and explain what are the 3 advantages to each of these lessons.

1.

    a.

    b.

    c.

2.

    a.

    b.

    c.

3.

      a.

      b.

      c.

Journal

Write about someone who bothers you. Do their actions trigger anger, sadness, or frustration? Explain what you can learn from an interaction with them.

How can you turn a negative situation into a bigger lesson on human nature?

TIP #15

You Can Plan and Achieve Your Dreams

Are you dreaming big enough? Do you have a written plan for some of your dreams? Your dreams are your responsibility alone; therefore, every action or non-action will bring you one step closer to your dreams or keep you at a stand still.

Your dreams are goals and visions that release joy into your heart every time you think about them. Dreams are designed to guide us towards our destiny and away from alignment with things that drain our energy, like bullies.

Your purpose for living is wrapped up in your dreams. Every thought will bring you closer or further from it. Feeling low often is associated with not knowing how to achieve your dreams.

Asking questions would be the first step in connecting with the dream you have inside of you. Aligning with your dreams would be impossible without asking yourself questions about what dreams you would like to pursue. Who do you need to connect with for making your dreams come true or what can you do now to start creating your dream?

Yvonne Brooks and Stephanie R. Bien, LMFT, LPCC

Without proactive questions going through your mind about your dreams, you cannot go any further.

The most crucial question to ask is, "how do I know I have chosen the right dream?" You know you have chosen the right dream because it connects you magnetically to the experience.

When a dream is right, it's impossible to let go of. The right dreams are usually big and challenging because they force you to increase your capacity in areas that you never thought of before just so you can expand your light on the earth.

Dreams that are bigger than your limited imagination are good indicators that you have come face to face with something that will change your life and the life of others for the better.

Only you can plan and achieve your goals. Waiting for someone to motivate you is not recommended. We are all waiting to see what big dreams you will create in your lifetime. Don't let us wait too long!

"Achieve" Questions to Ponder:

1. If you could do ANYTHING, what would that be?
2. How would self confidence improve your life?
3. What if you had a concrete plan for teenage life?
4. What if you had a written plan for after high school?
5. How would creating a teen success blueprint impact your life?

Solution

Every dream began with a thought. Allowing yourself to dream big is the practice of meditating on a flow of thoughts connected to the same subject matter.

Your thoughts are linked to your focus. Whatever you focus on, you are creating. You might not see it in the physical, but trust me you are getting ready to give birth to what you have been focusing on (positive or negative). We do this all the time. Our current state of mind is linked to our focused thoughts - conscious or unconscious.

Every focus has a vibration. Big dreams have stronger vibrations, meaning it will take more powerful thoughts to bring it into manifestation. It's easy to focus on a negative thought of hurting someone. It takes work to focus on positive ideas for taking control of your life and helping others.

It is within your power to choose to dream big, ask questions and practice a flow of positive thoughts for achieving your dreams. You have the power to plan and achieve your dreams – just look around to see proof. Many people such as Oprah Winfrey, Walt Disney, Malala (the teen girl from Pakistan who was shot in the face for advocating education for girls) and others have paid a heavy price for achieving big dreams.

This world is so blessed to have you. I know that there is something very powerful and empowering deep inside of you waiting to come out. So many people are waiting for what you will create to make a difference. I am excited about your future. Please share your big dream with us all.

Quotes

"A dream doesn't become reality through magic;
it takes sweat, determination and hard work."

~Colin Powell

"All our dreams come through,
if we have the courage to pursue them."

~Walt Disney

"The future belongs to those who believe in
the beauty of their dreams."

~Eleanor Roosevelt

"Dreams are today's answers to tomorrow's questions."

~Edgar Cayce

Practice

Write down a list of dreams that keep coming back to your mind. When you write down your dreams, it forces you to keep focus.

1._____

2._____

3._____

Pick one dream to maintain focus

_____

Set a deadline to accomplish the focused dream

_____

Write down your top three actions to move closer to manifestation of your dream.

1._____

2._____

3._____

Yvonne Brooks and Stephanie R. Bien, LMFT, LPCC

Journal

When I have a dream, I...

My biggest dream is to....

TIP#16

Find Something In Your Life That You Love, That You're Good At, And Do It!

So much time is spent on things you "have" to do, like going to class, doing homework, studying, doing chores, returning calls or texts and so much more.

To balance out life, it helps to have something that you feel joy from. The options are endless. Just a few ideas are participating in sports like basketball or surfing or learning a hobby like photography or dance, or volunteering by working with animals at a shelter or cleaning up a beach if you like to spend time outdoors.

By doing something you love, this feeds your soul, enhances your self-esteem and brings purpose to your life. The energy that comes out of this passion helps us to push through the things you "have to" do. It's like having a checking account. If you are spending and spending without depositing, you will end up broke, but if you spend energy, refuel a bit on activities that you enjoy, spend more and refuel again, your account will always remain full. We are like this as well - we need to balance work and fun. The best way to refuel is by doing what brings us joy, fulfillment and self-confidence.

This confidence is like a shield to protect us. Feeling good about ourselves, keeps us safe against the potential hurt that comes our way from bullying, judgment, criticism or just from making a mistake. Confidence can help you feel good about yourself, giving an opportunity of joy and internal peace.

"Happiness" Questions to Ponder:

1. What brings you positive energy?
2. How can you find this healthy activity that brings you pure joy?
3. Where would you put this into your schedule?
4. What percentage of time is spent on "have to's"?
5. If there were no financial or time restrictions, what would you do?

Solution

You may know exactly what you love and are good at. Great! Then go for it. If you aren't sure, you'll need to explore some ideas. If you're an outdoor person you might want to search online for outdoor activities and try a few. If you are more of a homebody, maybe you can teach yourself an instrument, write a song or learn yoga. Whatever it is, it must be something that brings you joy and that comes naturally to you.

Think back to when you were younger. What did you love to do? What did you want to do as much as possible? This can be a starting place. This can direct you to a type of fun. Was it an activity outside? Or inside? Was it physical? Or quiet? With many people or alone?

Finding your passion may be more challenging. Some exploration can be useful. Searching online can be helpful. Try talking to people of all ages and see how their energy and excitement changes when they speak about their desired activity. These are all ways to search for the one true joy that makes you feel alive.

Quotes

"Every great dream, begins with a dreamer. Always remember, you have within you the strength, the patience, and the passion to reach for the stars to change the world."

~Harriet Tubman

"We can each define ambition and progress for ourselves. The goal is to work toward a world where expectations are not set by the stereotypes that hold us back, but by our personal passion, talents and interests."

~Sheryl Sandberg

"Today is life - the only life you are sure of. Make the most of today. Get interested in something. Shake yourself awake. Develop a hobby. Let the winds of enthusiasm sweep through you. Live today with gusto."

~Dale Carnegie

"My hobbies include maintaining my physical and mental health. It's a full time job. Yoga definitely helps for both of them. I'm a big fan of relaxing and not having a schedule. That's my best way to keep from going crazy."

~Olivia Thirlby

Practice

Please think about the questions below, and then write the answers. This will give you insights and possibly a new perspective of life.

Write 3 things you enjoy doing or think you might be passionate about.

1.

2.

3.

Take one of the above ideas and make a plan of how you can do this. Set up a time and a place and decide which items you may need to implement this potential passion.

Journal

My friend is passionate about something and this is what it looks like…

Think back to a time when you had a hobby or passion and did it. Write about it…

TIP #17

Self Care Is An Important Ingredient In Life

Your relationship with yourself is foundational for your relationship with others. Caring for yourself with patience and mercy will inspire you to do the same for your family, friends and your community.

Placing a high priority in setting goals and taking action to care for your physical, mental, emotional and spiritual health is the highest standard of self-care.

Self-care is the quickest way to keep your emotional bank account filled up. The more you pay attention to how you feel about life and set goals to eliminate the thoughts that produce negative feelings, the greater your chances of maintaining a well-stocked emotional bank account.

Feeling tired, anxious, rushed, and impatient are a few of the symptoms that show up when self-care is deficient. The inability to implement a plan to care for yourself at a higher standard sets you up for a deficient emotional bank account. It puts you at the same level of bullies who are also deficient. The bullies are empty and looking for a quick fix of negative energy.

Bullies operate at a low frequency due to lack of self-care. If your emotional bank account is full, they will not be able to vibrate in your atmosphere. Once you get good at self-care and once you get used to vibrating at a high level, even if you are having an off day, you will have the tools to move quickly to a higher level of thought when you need to remove toxic situations and people from your life.

Self-care is a personal experience that only you can orchestrate. It is a mindset that focuses on being a better person so as to share your gifts with the world.

Working hard on yourself so that you can give quality communication and relationships to others is the key for living a fulfilled and happy life.

Establishing a sense of wellness from the inside out will always raise your frequency to experience relationships that vibrate the same back to you.

"Self-Care" Questions to Ponder:

1. What are some ideas for taking responsibility for your growth and development?
2. How can you improve caring for yourself?
3. What health condition would you like to be in?
4. If you could care more about yourself, where would you start?
5. How low will you allow yourself to go before caring about how you feel?

Solution

Self-care is not a one-time thing. It is a daily commitment to feeling your best. Nothing is done without first feeling it. Your greatest goal in self-care is to work diligently on feeling good as often as possible.

Feeling good about your physical life could begin with complimenting yourself. Keep track of the nice things people say about you and review it weekly or when you need a little encouragement.

Create an appreciation list for your entire body from the top of your head to the sole of your feet. Review this list as often as you need it.

Feeling good about your mental life involves taking time to relax, meditate and welcome peace to saturate your mind throughout your day. Invest time in increasing the value you give to others by shutting off the phone for an hour or so, just to entertain peace.

Use your imagination to create images of tranquility for at least ten minutes daily to care for your mind in a way that empowers you for greater good.

Feeling good about your emotional life involves paying attention to how you are feeling from the time you wake up until the time you go to bed. Make sure you are doing things from a position of feeling strong and that you're not in victim mode.

Your feelings are indicators that give you insight into the truth about your situation. Feeling good (peaceful) about a situation or a person is a sign of safety. Feeling fear, anxiety or stress are indicators that you are not in a healthy place to communicate to that person or work on that project. Take a break, regroup and return to the situation or the person with a healthier mindset.

Feeling good about your life is a part of your spirituality as it is about raising your consciousness. What type of life would you like to experience while you're still on planet Earth?

Make sure the thoughts you allow into your mind about how you should be living are yours alone. Embrace only positive thoughts about your potentials, your character, your possibilities and your success. The choice will always be yours.

Quote

"Take care of your body. It's the only place you have to live."
~Jim Rohn

"Don't be afraid to give your best to what seemly are small jobs.
Every time you conquer one it makes you that much stronger.
If you do the little jobs well, the big ones will tend to
take care of themselves."
~Dale Carnegie

"Women in particular need to keep an eye on their
physical and mental health, because if they are scurrying to and
from appointments and errands, we don't have a lot of time
to take care of ourselves. We need to do a better job
ourselves higher on our own "to do" list."
~Michelle Obama

"Love only seeks one thing: the good of the one loved.
It leaves the other secondary effects to take care of themselves.
Love therefore, is its own reward."
~Thomas Merton

Practice

Please think about the questions below, and then write the answers. This will give you ideas to make positive changes in your life.

Write down three goals you would like to add to your physical self-care routine within the next 90 days.

1._____

2._____

3._____

Write down three goals you would like to add to your mental self-care routine within the next 90 days.

1._____

2._____

3._____

Write down three goals you would like to add to your emotional self-care routine within the next 90 days.

1._____

2._____

3._____

Write down three goals you would like to add to your spiritual self-care routine within in the next 90 days.

1._____

2._____

3._____

Journal

To me, self-care means…

After reading this chapter, I chose to….

TIP #18

Have Balance in Your Life

Creating a balanced life takes focus and commitment to managing your emotional highs and lows. Your emotions are the best indicators for knowing how to have balance in your life.

Your emotional highs (allowing your feelings to guide you from the inside) through appreciation are indicators that you have the energy available to work on your projects, deal with challenging situations and take control of negative situations without effort.

Taking time at the beginning of each day to appreciate the many experiences of joy waiting for you, is an excellent start for setting the standard for how you will embrace life.

Appreciate the opportunities, the challenges, the relationships in your life. Appreciate your family, your teachers, your community and the value you bring to it all.

Appreciate your courage and determination to never give up. Appreciate your style of thinking, your sense of humor, the little things and the big things. Learn to invest time just appreciating the beauty and essence of who you are and the life you are a part of.

Your emotional lows (allowing outside situations to decide how you feel) are indicators to take a break. This is not the time to make decisions, study or deal with stressful situations. This is the perfect moment to go for a walk, take a nap or just stay in silence to refresh back to an emotional state of calmness.

Imbalance will only happen when you allow people (bullies), situations and things to decide how you are feeling. Imbalance is also your sign of personal neglect.

You are the only one that has the power to decide if you will or will not live a balanced life. Creating a life of balance is a decision, not a chore. Choose wisely.

"Balance" Questions to Ponder:

1. What does balance look like to you?
2. What if you had balance in your life?
3. How will being balanced affect your life?
4. If you were balanced, where would you invest your energy?
5. What steps will you take today to discover the benefits of being balanced?

Solution

Having a balanced life takes place in three dimensions: spirit, soul and body. Having too much time spent in one area can cause an imbalance. The goal is to invest time in all three areas daily so as to achieve maximum results for your day.

Spiritual balance consists of taking time to express gratitude and taking time for solitude. The perfect time to practice your spiritual balance is early in the morning. Write in your journal, read an inspirational book, pray, give thanks, take deep breaths, meditate, practice solitude and create a habit of leaving your home vibrating at your highest self.

Soul balance consists of managing your emotional highs and lows with skill. Paying attention to how you are feeling is much easier if you began your day with some form of spiritual balance. You will be more tuned into an emotional frequency that vibrates back to you what you deposited before you left home. No time for spiritual balance means your soul will also be out of balance. A balanced soul is a happy and calm soul, not a grumpy, worried or easily angered one.

Body balance consists of motivating yourself to get to school on time, study, do homework, engage with family and have a social life, and it is also caring and resting your body. One of the easiest things a balanced teen will experience is having self-control. Self-control is the end result of teenagers who have invested time in their spiritual, soul and body balance. The balance you will experience comes from making a decision to take responsibility at the beginning of your day for how you will live your life.

Spiritual, soul and body balance are critical for the development of a teenager's life. It is the heart of your existence. Without this balance, bullies will always have access.

Quotes

"I think there should be a good balance between being a good student and being able to enjoy your high school life."
~*Vanessa Minnillo*

"No person, no place and no thing have any power over us, for 'we' are the only thinkers in our mind. When we create peace and harmony and balance in our minds, we will find it in our lives."
~*Louise Hay*

"A lot of music is mathematics. It's balance."
~*Mel Brooks*

"Balance is good, because one extreme or the other leads to misery, and I've spent a lot of my life at one of those extremes."
~*Trent Reznor*

Practice

Please think about the questions below, and then write the answers. Be aware of the possibilities in your life and those around you.

Write down three spiritual habits you would like to develop within the next 30 days.

1._____

2._____

3._____

Write down three soul habits you would like to develop within the next 30 days.

1._____

2._____

3._____

Write down three body habits you would like to develop within the next 30 days.

1._____

2._____

3._____

Having a balanced life to me is....

Things I will appreciate more in my life include...

Conclusion

Learning the tools for how to take responsibility with being a teenager who refuses to be a victim to negative thoughts, emotions, people, situation and things demands commitment and character development.

Congratulations on taking the time to read Bully Prevention tips for teens. We are so proud of you!

Now it's time to celebrate with a friend, mentor or parent for the hard work you put in with investing time to add value to yourself.

You are now ready to share the tips you have learned about being bully free with your peers or anyone you know that is struggling with self-care.

We hope you will email us your story of how Bully Prevention Tips for Teens improved your life to <u>info@ brooksandbrooksfoundation.com</u> and qualify to win a $1000 scholarship for college. (Winners chosen in June)

Or visit amazon.com to give us a review.

To learn more about how to earn community service hours and make a difference in your community, please visit <u>www.brooksandbrooksfoundation.com</u>

Looking forward to hearing from you!

TEEN REFLECTION
THIRTY DAYS, SIX AND
TWELVE MONTH WORKSHEETS

How to Use the Teen Reflection-Thirty Days,
Six and Twelve Month Worksheets

Step One:

Complete reading the 18 Bully Prevention 4 Teens tips. Your main reason for completing this first is to get a clear idea of your current emotional state. This simple activity will put you in the position of operating at your highest emotional potential.

Step Two:

Take time to write down your progress with the 18 tips at the end of thirty days.

- Evaluate your results at the end of thirty days and write down your successes. Feedback is the only way of knowing your growth level.

Step Three:

Take time to write down your progress with the Bully Prevention 4 Teens Tips at your six month mark.

- Evaluate your results at the end of six months and write down your successes. Feedback is the only way of knowing your growth level.

Step Four:

Take time to write down your progress with the Bully Prevention 4 Teen Tips at your twelve month mark.

- Evaluate your results at the end of twelve months and write down your successes. Feedback is the only way of knowing your growth level.

TIP #1 REFLECTION-BELIEVE IN YOURSELF

How have you progressed in the past thirty days with believing in yourself?

_____

_____

_____

_____

_____

TIP #2 REFLECTION-ALIGN WITH YOUR PURPOSE FOR LIFE

How have you progressed in the past thirty days with aligning with your purpose for life?

_____

_____

_____

_____

_____

TIP #3 REFLECTION-WHAT OTHERS SAY CAN ONLY HURT YOU, IF YOU BELIEVE IT!

How have you progressed in the past thirty days with what others say about you?

_____

_____

_____

_____

_____

TIP #4 REFLECTION-LOOKING DEEPER INTO THE SOUL, AND UNDERSTANDING OTHERS!

How have you progressed in the past thirty days with looking deeper into your soul, and understanding others?

_____

_____

_____

_____

_____

TIP #5 REFLECTION-HOLDING ONTO ANGER LEADS TO UNHAPPINESS AND DARKNESS!

How have you progressed in the past thirty days with letting go of anger?

_____

_____

_____

_____

_____

TIP #6 REFLECTION-HAVE SPIRITUALITY IN YOUR LIFE!

How have you progressed in the past thirty days with having spirituality in your life?

_____

_____

_____

_____

_____

TIP #7 REFLECTION-BY GIVING TO OTHERS, YOU GET AS WELL!

How have you progressed in the past thirty days with giving to others?

_____

_____

_____

_____

_____

TIP #8 REFLECTION-POSITIVE ENERGY BRINGS ABOUT MORE POSITIVE ENERGY!

How have you progressed in the past thirty days with welcoming more positive energy?

_____

_____

_____

_____

_____

TIP #9 REFLECTION-TAKE A MOMENT TO BREATHE BEFORE REACTING!

How have you progressed in the past thirty days with taking moments to breathe before reacting?

_____

_____

_____

_____

_____

TIP #10 REFLECTION-ACCEPT AND LOVE YOURSELF!

How have you progressed in the past thirty days with accepting and loving yourself?

_____

_____

_____

_____

_____

TIP #11 REFLECTION-SPEAKING BADLY ABOUT ANOTHER BRINGS NEGATIVITY BACK TO YOU!

How have you progressed in the past thirty days with speaking only good about others?

_____

_____

_____

_____

_____

TIP #12 REFLECTION-WORRY ONLY WASTES TIME AND ENERGY!

How have you progressed in the past thirty days with worrying less?

_____

_____

_____

_____

TIP #13 REFLECTION-TAKE QUIET TIME DAILY EVEN IF IT'S ONLY FIVE MINUTES!

How have you progressed in the past thirty days with taking quiet time daily?

_____

_____

_____

_____

_____

TIP #14 REFLECTION-PAY ATTENTION ALL AROUND YOU. LISTEN TO EVERYONE, TEACHERS COME IN ALL SIZES AND FORMS!

How have you progressed in the past thirty days with paying attention to all around you?

_____

_____

_____

_____

_____

TIP #15 REFLECTION-YOU CAN PLAN AND ACHIEVE YOUR DREAMS!

How have you progressed in the past thirty days with planning and achieving your dreams?

_____

_____

_____

_____

_____

TIP #16 REFLECTION-FIND SOMETHING IN YOUR LIFE THAT YOU LOVE, AND DO IT!

How have you progressed in the past thirty days with finding something in life that you love, and doing it?

_____

_____

_____

_____

_____

TIP #17 REFLECTION-SELF-CARE IS AN IMPORTANT INGREDIENT IN LIFE!

How have you progressed in the past thirty days with putting self-care as a priority?

_____

_____

_____

_____

_____

TIP #18 REFLECTION-HAVE
BALANCE IN YOUR LIFE!

How have you progressed in the past thirty days with having balance in your life?

_____

_____

_____

_____

TEEN REFLECTION-SIX MONTHS

TIP #1 REFLECTION-BELIEVE IN YOURSELF

How have you progressed in the past six months with believing in yourself?

_____

_____

_____

_____

_____

TIP #2 REFLECTION-ALIGN WITH YOUR PURPOSE FOR LIFE!

How have you progressed in the past six months with aligning with your purpose for life?

_____

_____

_____

_____

_____

TIP #3 REFLECTION-WHAT OTHERS SAY CAN ONLY HURT YOU, IF YOU BELIEVE IT!

How have you progressed in the past six months with what others say about you?

_____

_____

_____

_____

TIP #4 REFLECTION-LOOKING DEEPER INTO THE SOUL AND UNDERSTANDING OTHERS!

How have you progressed in the past six months with looking deeper into your soul, and understanding others?

_____

_____

_____

_____

_____

TIP #5 REFLECTION-HOLDING ONTO ANGER LEADS TO UNHAPPINESS AND DARKNESS!

How have you progressed in the past six months with letting go of anger?

_____

_____

_____

_____

_____

TIP #6 REFLECTION-HAVE SPIRITUALITY IN YOUR LIFE!

How have you progressed in the past six months with having spirituality in your life?

_____

_____

_____

_____

_____

TIP #7 REFLECTION-BY GIVING TO OTHERS, YOU GET AS WELL!

How have you progressed in the past six months with giving to others?

_____

_____

_____

_____

_____

TIP #8 REFLECTION-POSITIVE ENERGY BRINGS ABOUT MORE POSITIVE ENERGY!

How have you progressed in the past six months with welcoming more positive energy?

_____

_____

_____

_____

_____

TIP #9 REFLECTION-TAKE A MOMENT TO BREATHE BEFORE REACTING!

How have you progressed in the past six months with taking moments to breathe before reacting?

_____

_____

_____

_____

TIP #10 REFLECTION-ACCEPT AND LOVE YOURSELF!

How have you progressed in the past six months with accepting and loving yourself?

_____

_____

_____

_____

_____

TIP #11 REFLECTION-SPEAKING BADLY ABOUT ANOTHER BRINGS NEGATIVITY BACK TO YOU!

How have you progressed in the past six months with speaking only good about others?

_____

_____

_____

_____

_____

TIP #12 REFLECTION-WORRY ONLY WASTES TIME AND ENERGY!

How have you progressed in the past six months with worrying less?

_____

_____

_____

_____

_____

TIP #13 REFLECTION-TAKE QUIET TIME DAILY EVEN IF IT'S ONLY FIVE MINUTES!

How have you progressed in the past six months with taking quiet time daily?

_____

_____

_____

_____

_____

TIP #14 REFLECTION-PAY ATTENTION ALL AROUND YOU. LISTEN TO EVERYONE... TEACHERS COME IN ALL SIZES AND FORMS!

How have you progressed in the past six months with paying attention to all around you?

_____

_____

_____

_____

_____

TIP #15 REFLECTION-YOU CAN PLAN AND ACHIEVE YOUR DREAMS!

How have you progressed in the past six months with planning and achieving your dreams?

_____

_____

_____

_____

_____

TIP #16 REFLECTION-FIND SOMETHING IN YOUR LIFE THAT YOU LOVE, AND DO IT!

How have you progressed in the past six months with finding something in life that you love, and doing it?

_____

_____

_____

_____

_____

TIP #17 REFLECTION-SELF-CARE IS AN IMPORTANT INGREDIENT IN LIFE!

How have you progressed in the past six months with putting self-care as a priority?

_____

_____

_____

_____

_____

TIP #18 REFLECTION-HAVE BALANCE IN YOUR LIFE!

How have you progressed in the past six months with having balance in your life?

_____

_____

_____

_____

_____

TEEN REFLECTION-TWELVE MONTHS

TIP #1 REFLECTION-BELIEVE IN YOURSELF

How have you progressed in the past twelve months with believing in yourself?

_____

_____

_____

_____

_____

TIP #2 REFLECTION-ALIGN WITH YOUR PURPOSE FOR LIFE!

How have you progressed in the past twelve months with aligning with your purpose for life?

_____

_____

_____

_____

_____

TIP #3 REFLECTION-WHAT OTHERS SAY CAN ONLY HURT YOU, IF YOU BELIEVE IT!

How have you progressed in the past twelve months with what others say about you?

_____

_____

_____

_____

_____

TIP #4 REFLECTION-LOOKING DEEPER INTO THE SOUL, AND UNDERSTANDING OTHERS!

How have you progressed in the past twelve months with looking deeper into your soul, and understanding others?

_____

_____

_____

_____

_____

TIP #5 REFLECTION-HOLDING ONTO ANGER LEADS TO UNHAPPINESS AND DARKNESS!

How have you progressed in the past twelve months with letting go of anger?

_____

_____

_____

_____

_____

TIP #6 REFLECTION-HAVE SPIRITUALITY IN YOUR LIFE!

How have you progressed in the past twelve months with having spirituality in your life?

_____

_____

_____

_____

_____

TIP #7 REFLECTION-BY GIVING TO OTHERS, YOU GET AS WELL!

How have you progressed in the past twelve months with giving to others?

_____

_____

_____

_____

_____

TIP #8 REFLECTION-POSITIVE ENERGY BRINGS ABOUT MORE POSITIVE ENERGY!

How have you progressed in the past twelve months with welcoming more positive energy?

_____

_____

_____

_____

_____

TIP #9 REFLECTION-TAKE A MOMENT TO BREATHE BEFORE REACTING!

How have you progressed in the past twelve months with taking moments to breathe before reacting?

_____

_____

_____

_____

_____

TIP #10 REFLECTION-ACCEPT AND LOVE YOURSELF!

How have you progressed in the past twelve months with accepting and loving yourself?

_____

_____

_____

_____

_____

Yvonne Brooks and Stephanie R. Bien, LMFT, LPCC

TIP #11 REFLECTION- SPEAKING BADLY ABOUT ANOTHER BRINGS NEGATIVITY BACK TO YOU!

How have you progressed in the past twelve months with speaking only good about others?

_____

_____

_____

_____

TIP #12 REFLECTION-WORRY ONLY
WASTES TIME AND ENERGY!

How have you progressed in the past twelve months with worrying less?

_____

_____

_____

_____

TIP #13 REFLECTION-TAKE QUIET TIME DAILY EVEN IF IT'S ONLY FIVE MINUTES!

How have you progressed in the past twelve months with taking quiet time daily?

_____

_____

_____

_____

_____

TIP #14 REFLECTION-PAY ATTENTION ALL AROUND YOU. LISTEN TO EVERYONE... TEACHERS COME IN ALL SIZES AND FORMS!

How have you progressed in the past twelve months with paying attention to all around you?

_____

_____

_____

_____

_____

TIP #15 REFLECTION-YOU CAN PLAN AND ACHIEVE YOUR DREAMS!

How have you progressed in the past twelve months with planning and achieving your dreams?

_____

_____

_____

_____

_____

TIP #16 REFLECTION-FIND SOMETHING IN YOUR LIFE THAT YOU LOVE, AND DO IT!

How have you progressed in the past twelve months with finding something in life that you love, and doing it?

_____

_____

_____

_____

_____

TIP #17 REFLECTION-SELF-CARE IS AN IMPORTANT INGREDIENT IN LIFE!

How have you progressed in the past twelve months with putting self-care as a priority?

_____

_____

_____

_____

_____

TIP #18 REFLECTION-HAVE BALANCE IN YOUR LIFE!

How have you progressed in the past twelve months with having balance in your life?

_____

_____

_____

_____

Suggested Resources

"The Four Agreements" by Don Miguel Ruiz

"The 7 Habits of Highly Effective Teens" by Stephen R. Covey

"The Surprising Purpose of Anger: Beyond Anger Management" by Marshall B. Rosenberg

"Bully, the Bullied, and the Not-So-Innocent Bystander" by Barbara Colorosa

"Bullying in Sports" by Randy Nathan, MSW

"Stress Management 4 Teens" by Yvonne Brooks

"Friendship: How to Make, Keep and Grow your Friendships" by Lauren Colhoun

Stopbullying.gov

Safekids.com

Thinkkindness.org

Yvonne Brooks has become known as the "Parenting with Love Coach." She is the industry leader in teaching parents about using love to decode their children's emotional language. She is the author of the best-selling book, **Building Your Child's Self-Esteem: 9 Secrets Parents Need to Know** and co-author of, **The Soul Repair Manual: Volume 1 – Self-Esteem**

Yvonne is the executive director of the **Brooks & Brooks Foundation**, a non-profit organization that serves, educates, and empowers families toward living with purpose.

Yvonne has over 25 years of experience as a parenting expert and she is the only parenting coach to create a ten-year parenting course that teaches parents step-by-step how to increase their children's capacity for emotional growth and development.

She has taught her award-winning workshop *"Understanding Your Child's Emotional Language"* to over 1,000 parents in public and private schools.

Yvonne is the creator of **Parenting with Love**, a series which teaches parents how to build stronger parent-child relationships through healthy communications that are rich in love. She has also created a **Parental Leadership Toolkit** to give parents additional resources to help their children and families become more successful.

As the number of families in need increased each year, Yvonne soon realized it would be crucial for her to attract other entrepreneurial women as well as executives from other organizations to partner with her. A master at finding win/win partnerships, Yvonne has dramatically increased the number of families being helped…all through the art of collaboration!

Yvonne Brooks credits her success to God and the wonderful people in her life. She lives in Los Angeles, California with her husband.

Stephanie R. Bien is a licensed Marriage, Family and Child therapist and licensed Professional Clinical Counselor with private practices in Agoura Hills and Calabasas, California. She specializes in psychotherapy, play therapy and parenting with children, teens and families to help with self esteem, stress, communication, school, social and family issues. She also teaches "Parent  Effectiveness Training" designed by Dr. Thomas Gordon, a three-time Nobel Peace Prize nominee and has had the honor of helping families for over 25 years. She is a community leader with many organizations including Brooks and Brooks Foundation for volunteer activities. Stephanie is the mother of 2 teen daughters as well. She has a passion for her work and life and tries to practice what she teaches by living a life of self-care, love, spirituality and peace.

Printed in the United States
By Bookmasters